I Love Mu

Mud is squishy.

Mud is sticky.

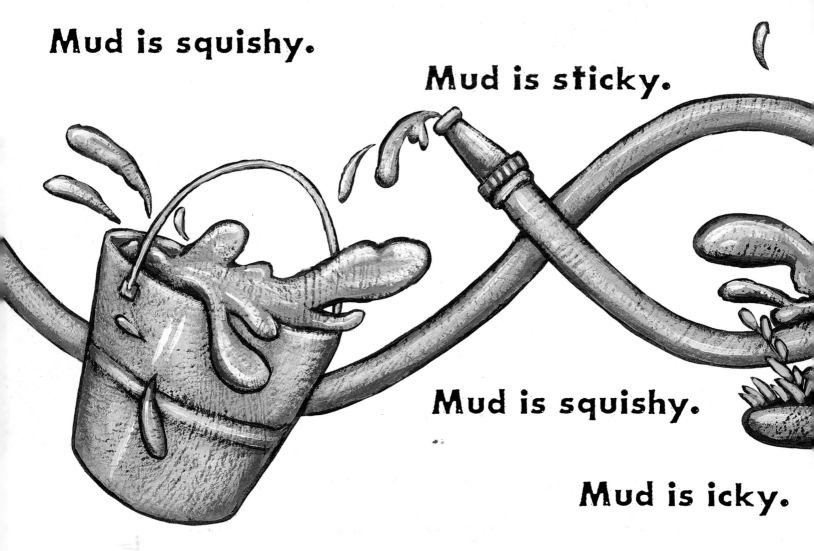

Mud is squishy.

Mud is icky.

I can make a big, big mess.
I like to play in mud the best!

Mud on my shoes.

Mud on my shirt.

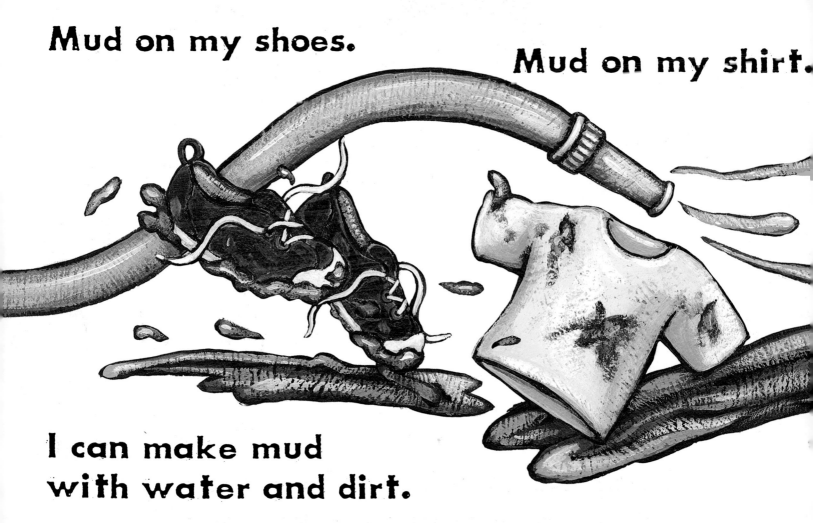

I can make mud
with water and dirt.

I can make a big, big mess.
I like to play in mud the best!

Jump in the mud.

Jump in the ooze.

Oh, lovely mud

in my hair, in my shoes.

I can make a big, big mess.
I like to play in mud the best!